ANCIENT HISTORY

haibun and tanka prose

Adelaide B. Shaw

ISBN: 978-81-19228-46-1

First Edition: 2023

Rs. 200/-

Cyberwit.net

HIG 45 Kaushambi Kunj, Kalindipuram

Allahabad - 211011 (U.P.) India

http://www.cyberwit.net

Tel: +(91) 9415091004

E-mail: info@cyberwit.net

Printed at VCORRE PRESS.

PREFACE

New Haven, Connecticut is my home town. The population when I was there—1936 to 1952— was over 160,000. It was not a small town, but my experiences growing up were centered around family and a small neighborhood of Italian, Irish, Polish, and Portuguese families.

This ancient history remembered here begins with my father and my mother and ends with the start of a new life 3,000 miles away.

These haibun and tanka prose are my fond recollections of an earlier time, neither simpler nor more difficult than the present, just different.

CONTENTS

DAD	9
MOM	11
GRANDPARENTS	14
THE OLD NEIGHBORHOOD	15
KINDERGARDEN—THE FIRST DAY	17
SEASONS OF WAR	19
SOLDIER BOY	21
A CHILDHOOD CHRISTMAS	22
A WINTER AFTERNOON	23
CRY BABY, CRY BABY	24
FAMILY TRIPS	25
THE LONG WAIT	26
BIG SISTER	27
SNOW DAY	28
SUNDAY MORNING WITH DAD	29
SUMMER NIGHTS	30
GRANDMA'S NOODLES	31
LIGHTS OUT	32
THE HAIRCUT	34
YOU GO FIRST	36
THE PALACE	37

RASCATTI'S BEACH	38
A SUNNER NIGHT WITH AUNT GERT	39
SQUABBLES	41
MUFFINS	42
NIGHT TERRORS	43
SPRING CLEANING	44
MOM'S WAFFLES	45
PARTNERS IN CRIME	46
SUMMER OF 1944	47
TRAPPED	48
WINE HARVEST	49
BLACKIE	50
THE FIVE AND DIME	51
FABLES AND OTHER YARNS	52
TREASURE	53
LUNCH WITH GRANDMA AND GRANDPA	54
GIVE ME ENTERTAINMENT	56
NINE LIVES	57
THAT WONDERFUL TOWN	58
COUSINS	60
CENTER STAGE	62
REMNANTS	63
WHAT I DID LAST SUMMER	64

AN INTRODUCTION 66
SINGING THE CHRISTMAS MASS 68
BEST FRIENDS 70
THE SOCK HOP 71
ARRIVERDERCI 72
ACKNOWLEDGEMENTS 73

DAD

He is a Neapolitan child of the streets, in short pants and skinned knees, until he is apprenticed to a tailor and learns how to handle a needle and thread, how to cut cloth, how, with wool or silk or gabardine, to take arms and legs, torso and shoulders, and reshape them into a new man.

> moldering leaves
> spread on the forest floor
> hidden mushrooms

In 1908, at age eighteen, with only a few lira, his scissors and thimble in his pocket, he leaves behind a struggling family in a town often layered with the ashes of Vesuvius. He travels in steerage, twelve days in the bowels of the ship before docking in Boston harbor.

> falling snow—
> faces on the gangway
> turn upward

From Boston to New York. A crowded coach train, standing all the way. The address of his brother securely pinned in the inner pocket of his jacket.

> tramping through snow—
> one street like another
> yet all different

The universal language of craft lands him a job. Other countrymen with their needles and thread sew together a strong bond. He settles in, adjusting to the cold, throbbing city. A city not paved with gold, but covered with snow and garbage and teaming with the human throng. He claims a place in a corner of his brother's apartment, in the community of tailors, in the New World.

signs of spring—
tenement buildings
sprout window boxes

MOM

Nonna's House

A small house in the hills. Rough gray stone. A vegetable patch in the back. A few orange trees on the side. Nonno is away again, somewhere in the hills, hauling his wagon of water barrels to different villages. He has his mastiff for company and protection against bandits. Nonna has Lucia. She is 10 years old.

moonlight
shining on her beads
she counts off the prayers

Her chores are to gather kindling, feed the chickens, sweep the floor, get milk from the goat boy.

bells in the wind
kids follow their dams
over rocks

spring blossoms
a clean straw mattress
free from bugs

In the afternoon she studies her catechism. Recites it for Nonna.

First Communion
after a cleansing rain
the festive table

The visits end. She is leaving. It is February 1917

sea and clouds
between sleep and waking
a life imagined

The Voyage

Steerage, the lowest area for passengers. Men on one side. Women and children on the other. She is crossing with her mother, two younger brothers and a baby sister. The New World waiting. Her father, an older brother and two older sisters waiting. She is 13.

A narrow iron framed bunk bed, one of a hundred in a long room. Two swinging lanterns overhead. A thin mattress, a skimpy blanket and life preserver on every bunk.

Life on board consists of long lines for food, for the toilet, for washing. Stale, smelly air below; clean, brisk and cold air on deck. Now and then a treat.

a fresh orange
three sections for herself
to slowly savor
each bite a memory
of Nonna's tree

On the third day out an alarm. Life jackets put on. The waiting on deck, perhaps to all die. The engine stilled. U-boats. Torpedoes. New words. New fears.

Every day, always the rocking and swaying, always the confinement, the restlessness, the wish to run across the hills again.

sea spray on the wind
a slow walk around deck
and back
the ache in her legs
moves to her heart

After 16 days the flat horizon changes shape. Land. An island, a statue high on a pedestal holding a torch. She stands on deck in falling snow. The first she has ever seen.

fragile and light
flakes on her open hand
quickly melt;
fragile and light all her dreams
shadowed in the dawn

GRANDPARENTS

A box of photos saved from my parents' house. In one photo an old couple stands close together. The man has a thick, white mustache and a bald head; the woman has white hair pulled tightly into a bun, an ample bosom and wide hips. Stiff and formal in the black and white picture. The stern faces give a lie to what I know.

afternoon rocking-
the odors of food
and warm flesh

They feed us, scold us, hug us. Italian immigrants. Few English words understood and even fewer spoken. Never mind.

hand and hand–
from the tobacco shop
to the ice cream store

Within a few months of each other they are gone. Too young to understand, too old to forget.

relatives gather-
another party with tears
and stories

THE OLD NEIGHBORHOOD

Summer

As a child, I am unaware of the differences between working class and rich. One fourth of our yard is given to vegetables, one fourth to grass and a clothesline, one half to a grape arbor. Under the thick vines, pieces of linoleum placed over the hard packed dirt. A rusty metal table and wobbly chairs where Grandma sits shelling peas or mending, Grandpa, drinking a glass of wine made from his own grapes. My older sister and I playing jacks or checkers.

My street is "my street." Factories on one side and houses on the other.

> Good Year Rubber smells
> adding weight to the hot air–
> lemonade for sale

The factory walls – good for throwing balls against on summer evenings.

> on the front porch
> making paper fans—
> the tinkle of ice

Autumn.

Grandpa making wine in the cellar. The air, sweet and heady.

> bees circling
> the full baskets of grapes
> snatching a bunch

Winter.

Watching coal slide down a chute, dust peppering our faces. The furnace, huge and black with a dragon's mouth. Grandpa stokes it, working in his undershirt, bare arms glowing, beads of sweat on his bald head.

wet mittens
drying on the radiator
the smell of burnt wool

Spring.

It slips into the small gardens. Lilacs and tulips. A lightness in the air.

skipping to school–
lily of the valley
for the teacher

KINDERGARTEN–THE FIRST DAY

Outside the classroom door, I hesitate, unsure, anxious. Softly crying, “I want to go home.”

Inside, a young teacher. Slender, soft voice, pretty hair, pretty dress. Still… “ I want to go home.”

“All mothers must leave. It will be fine.”

No. Not fine. “ WANT…TO…GO…HOME!"

"Stop that or you'll get a spanking."

I don’t like her. She’s shaking me and she’s *not* pretty. My new shoes slip across the floor as she pulls me to a place on the rug.

“Noooooooo…..”

The other children, all looking. Beginning to sniffle, whimper, cry. Getting louder. I’m louder still.

“HOME…WANT TO GO HOME!”

"Come here!"

A different voice. Deeper. Older. A giant in a dark dress. Stiff gray hair pulled back and steel gray eyes behind steel-rimmed glasses. She’s pulling me to the front of the room, to a chair where she sits. Lifting me up and over her knees. A brown leather strap in her hand, like Grandpa uses to sharpen his razor. One Whack! Across my bottom.

"Are you going to stop that noise?” she asks, “Or do you want another spanking?"

Silence from the other children. The giant and I look at each other. I don’t like her, either, but I say nothing. Sniff back the mucus and rub tears from my face. And still say nothing. All morning, I say nothing.

Just before school is over, a summons to the principal's office. The giant again, sitting at a large desk. "For being a good girl the rest of the morning,” she says.

bouquet of flowers –
small hands hold tightly
the wet stems

SEASONS OF WAR

Church in the early morning; a stop at the bakery for fresh rolls; roller skating in front of the house. The beginning of an ordinary Sunday in our New England town.

December cold
rippling through the neighborhood
news of Pearl Harbor

Within weeks our lives change. No butter, no meat, no short-wave radio. At night, surprise black-outs. Listening in the dark to the block warden's footsteps approach and fade away.

the windows open—
supper by moonlight
until the all clear

My mother works now. The swing shift at the mill, weaving olive drab and khaki.

rain in the air—
raking leaves with Grandpa
after school

As the months and years pass, we develop new games. No more playing cowboys and Indians. We become army nurses, bomber pilots, soldiers with machine guns.

snowballs fly—
everyone wants to be
on the winning side

At home, the talk is often heavy with long pauses. Frequent mention of an uncle in Naples, the cousins in Sicily. We have shortages, but they have even less. We send packages: blankets, clothing, canned goods. Our prayers are longer.

A sameness settles in; even war has a familiar routine. Another bond drive; a new scrap drive. Nothing wasted and everything saved; make-do and make over. "It's the war" becomes the explanation for everything.

Victory Garden—
more buggy tomatoes
on the ground

SOLDIER BOY

Uncle Jimmie lives downstairs with my grandparents and Aunt Gert. He sleeps on a daybed in the parlor and is fair game to torment and pester when he is sleeping late on the weekends. I poke him, tickle him and try to pry open his eyelids. He is good-natured, gives me piggy-back rides, draws me cartoons. He torments me in turn by calling me Addie Pie, a name that sticks for far too long. In the spring of 1942, he is drafted.

Worry about him is constant. Each day the wait for a V-mail letter, and when it comes, unable to read any meaning between censored words. and blotches.

the neighbor's lilacs—
a teasing hint of fragrance
on the breeze

Comes home when the war is over and sleeps again in the parlor. He is quieter, doesn't talk about the war. I no longer pester him.

homecoming
the fading echoes
of another time

A CHILDHOOD CHRISTMAS

This is a time of joy, of pleasure in anticipation. The lights and sparkle, the fragrances and food. The snow and presents.

December is the longest month in my impatient child mind. The days of Advent. Count them off–one, two, three…days of diligently working on the embroidered pillow cases for Aunt Jo, the making of paper chains and snowflakes, of sponge painting plain tissue to use as gift wrap, of helping Mom bake cookies and fruitcake.

There are trips into town to view the decorated windows, visits to toy land and Santa. It doesn't matter that department store Santas are seldom plump and rolly-polly, but often thin and angular. We know they are stand-ins for the real Santa who is busy working in the North Pole. This is a time to accept, to believe and hope, a time to wish, to ignore the news of the dead and dying, of battles won and lost in Europe and in the Pacific, a time to not speak of Uncle Jim fighting somewhere in Italy, a time not to complain about shortages, about Dad working late, about Mom working the swing shift from four to eleven p.m.

evening prayers
I forget to put myself
at the end

A WINTER AFTERNOON

The kitchen at dusk. A soft bubbling from the pot on the back burner. An old man at the table. His full stomach keeps the chair several inches away. A merry face. Pink with a full white mustache. On his equally pink bald head is a black knit cap.

He pours dark red wine made from his own grapes, sips, smacks his lips. Now a glass for me, much smaller, watered down, befitting my size. I copy him, dip a chunk of stale bread in my wine. It dissolves in my mouth to nothing. Tangy juices spurt down my throat and my chin. The old man, my grandfather, wipes my dribbles with his handkerchief. I am five years old.

steam covered windows—
a snow carrying wind
rattles the back gate

CRY BABY, CRY BABY

Because she's chubby and doesn't run fast. Because she can't throw or catch well. Because she is shy. Because she is easily hurt. Because she'd rather be chosen last than stay home alone with no one to play with.

Halloween
a real princess hides
beneath the costume

FAMILY TRIPS

Summer vacation, as a young child in New Haven, means days spent on the schoolyard, a local playground or on neighborhood streets. When my father isn't too tired, outings by trolley to the beach on Sunday or to the amusement park at Savin Rock in West Haven. A supper of fried clams, soft shell crab or pizza ends the day.

Overnight trips away are rare and short. The occasional one-night stay-over in New York City to see the Rockets at Radio City Music Hall or a relative's wedding in the Bronx.

The longest trip we take is a week-long vacation with my mother's older sister and her husband. My uncle drives the six of us to the Desert of Maine. We share a two-room cabin, my parents, my sister and I in one room, my aunt and uncle in another.

I am four and my sister six and neither of us is diplomatic regarding the arrangements made by my aunt and uncle. The cabin is too small. Why is there a sink in one bedroom, a cooking stove and ice-box in the other? Why are the toilet and shower outside? The sand is too hot. I want to go home.

We whine and my aunt nags. She nags her husband, my mother, my sister and me. For some reason she leaves my father alone.

shifting dunes
the lone man takes
a new direction

THE LONG WAIT

I am eight years old and in the hospital for a tonsillectomy. Knowing that there is something in my throat which is often making me sick and that once removed I will feel better does not lesson my fears. But, I am a brave little girl. Or pretend to be. I'm not sure, but I don't cry or whimper or protest when the nurse leads me away from my mother.

On a rolling bed, I'm wheeled into a too bright room, all white and shiny, with silvery tables and cabinets. Men and women in masks fuss around me talking, talking. I understand nothing except "Breathe into the cup and count backwards from one hundred. "Ninety-nine, ninety-eight, ninety-seven… nine…

The room in which I wake is dimly lighted. The girl in the bed next to me is crying; another child across the aisle in calling, "Mama," just the very word I want to say, but can't. I don't feel better as I was told. My throat hurts. I want the pain to go away. I want to go home. I want…I want…

waiting for mama
in a hospital gown
little girl lost

waiting for mama
the little girl cries
as she wets herself

waiting for mama
the little girl swallows pain
and chocolate ice cream

BIG SISTER

She teases and torments me; plays with me and protects; chases me away and calls me back.

We share a room, toys and clothes, sickness and secrets. We fight, yell and scream, scratch and pinch. I bite her once. The taste of brown soap still remembered. When she's away at camp I'm lonely.

She explains important matters. The "curse," an aunt's growing stomach, how boys are different from girls, why a neighbor divorced her husband.

sticky night
whispering
after lights out

SNOW DAY

The radio announcer declares at 7:00 a.m. that all schools are closed. There is no movement except for the snow. The gray light and falling snow obscure the neighborhood. Our street is seen as if in a shifting dream. There are no factories across from us, no chain link fences, no broken concrete and blacktop, no parked cars. Only snow. Mounds of snow. A bale of cotton wadding of snow. A whipped cream cake of snow. A giant marshmallow of snow.

a ragged path
the scrape of my shovel
sharply clear

SUNDAY MORNING WITH DAD

I'm a young child–five years old, six, seven. My sister, two years older. It is mid-winter, high summer, any and all seasons. We wait with Dad on the corner for the trolley. My sister and I in our best dresses. Dad in a suit.

We get off in the center of town at The Green. Dad buys peanuts. Some for us, some for the pigeons. We chase them. Dad attracts them. They land on his hat, his shoulder. They eat out of his hand.

"Stand still," he says. "Wait and they will come."

Sunday church bells
summoning the faithful
a flurry of pigeons

Dad is soon joined by other men, other custom tailors for "shop talk." These other tailors leave their children at home. A few hours of escape, peace. Not Dad. Proud and pleased he is. Our clean faces and healthy bodies. Our freshly pressed clothes sewn by Mom, our smart coats tailored by his hands. Having married late, at age 45, he likes to show off his young daughters. Most of the time we oblige, knowing there may be a stop at Clark's Dairy Bar before going home.

sun on her face
the little girl sneezes
at the tall stranger

SUMMER NIGHTS

Families on their front porches. Grandma with a paper fan. Grandpa and Dad with cold beers. Mom with hot coffee, regardless of the heat. My sister and I–cream soda, out of the bottle. Wet and slippery in our grimy hands. Sweet and bubbly and cool. One gulp. Then another. Then settling into a slow sipping, making it last until bedtime.

circling moths
under a street lamp
the last game of jacks

GRANDMA'S NOODLES

She has flour up to her elbows. With sturdy hands she kneads the dough, pressing against the soft mass and pushing down and forward. Gives it a quarter turn and repeats the process until the dough is no longer sticky, but smooth. She lets it rest.

the mantle clock
pinging the quarter hour–
suddenly awake

She punches down the dough, rolls it out to a quarter inch thickness. With a sharp knife, cuts thin strips, places them on a floured sheet spread across the bed. By dinner time, the chicken has been stewed and the broth is at the boil, ready for the dry noodles. Grandpa and I watch and wait with our empty bowls.

steam covered window
I draw a heart
with no name

LIGHTS OUT

My older sister and I sit in the kitchen in the dark, listening to the radio. A squeaking door, heavy footsteps. Goose bumps appear on my arms.

'Turn the lights on," I say.

"No. It's spookier with them off."

A chicken heart, fallen on the ground still beats.

Thump-th-thump.

It becomes louder and larger, engulfing the town, the country, the entire world. I want to leave…yet, I stay.

THUMP-TH-THUMP.

After the program, I go shakily to bed.

"Scaredy-cat, scaredy-cat."

"Mommmmieeee."

"Stop teasing your sister."

Thump-th-thump.

It's beating on the floor across the room.

"Stop that." I *know* it's my sister, but…still…

Thump-th-thump.

A deep voice, slow and pulsating, the same words over and over. I burrow under the blankets.

"Chiiiickennn hearrrrt….."

hazy heat
nothing to do
but follow sis

THE HAIRCUT

It's my sister's fault. We both have long hair. Mom keeps it off our faces with barrettes . Mary Lou fidgets all the time with her hair, twisting a shank around and around her fingers. Pops it into her mouth. Mom braids it. Now she has a convenient shank of hair to gnaw on. A reminder to stop doesn't work. Scolding doesn't work. A slap on the hand doesn't work.

The hot, sticky summer gets hotter with daily battles. One morning, while out shopping with Mom, Mary Lou's at it again. Hair in her mouth. Sucking. Slurping. Mom sees the solution in front of her. She pulls us into the barber shop, and Mary Lou gets a haircut. Not just a trim. A CUT. Short as a boy's. She doesn't cry or whine, but sits in the barber's chair with her lips clamped shut and her eyes squinting.

I'm happily swiveling around in the next chair until a white cloth drops around me and the barber gives me a matching haircut. It's not fair. I don't chew my hair. But, it's done and I cry all the way home.

That afternoon, wearing overalls and tee shirt, I'm alone on our front porch.

"Go home, little boy. You don't belong here." My aunt doesn't recognize me, and I begin to cry again.

I don't know why I was sheared. Maybe, it was to prevent me from the habit. Maybe, to keep Mary Lou from feeling alone. Years later, Mom admits she doesn't know why.

parents and children—
a learning experience
for everyone
with luck, time softens the hurts
and sweetens the joys

YOU GO FIRST

Grandpa's cellar. Musty and dank. Mary Lou and I don't like it. The lingering musk in the wine press. Scant light from two small windows splotched with mud. Dark corners where anything could hide. Spiders, mice, dead or alive. Grandma's jarred fruits and vegetables on warped shelves draped in snarling webs. The coal burning furnace throwing off heat and smells.

preserved peaches
four small hands
to retrieve one jar

THE PALACE

Long ago there was a fairy tale palace. Very grand in size. Everywhere one looked– velvet, gold and bronze. Mirrored walls, crystal chandeliers and thick carpets. Stairways wide enough to hold six abreast. Sweeping in a curve, they rise up toward a domed ceiling with a glass skylight.

A princess comes down the stairs. Regal, beautiful, bedecked in glimmering jewels, wearing her best dress and Sunday shoes. Her subjects bow.

"Your Royal Highness," they murmur as she passes.

"Out of my way, peasants," she says, moving past them towards the palace doors.

"Come on, come on," says a page wearing blue pants and a jacket with gold braid. He gruffly hurries the princess outside and ushers in those waiting for the next scheduled movie.

the walk home–
squinting in the low sunlight
she scuffs her shoes

RASCATTI'S BEACH

Mid-summer. A sharp briny smell coming from drying seaweed and ocean breezes. Located just outside New Haven, it's not a popular spot, this remote stretch along Long Island Sound. On a promontory overlooking the ocean, a few rough tables and benches under a lattice enclosure at one end; at the other, a primitive outhouse with half-moon cutouts for ventilation. At the bottom of a stone stairway, a narrow beach that disappears with the tide.

sand castle–
the moat returns
to the sea

Italian families, the same ones, come year after year. Usually just our family and one other. You can hear the ocean at Rascatti's. No competing sounds from radios, food vendors, no kids kicking sand and throwing balls. No lifeguards, either. Just the rhythmic splash of waves on rocks, the slurp of water withdrawing, the brush of the wind through trees, the cries of gulls. My father's favorite beach. The kind of beach I didn't appreciate then, but would enjoy now.

game of checkers—
a latticed sunburn
on his bare back

A SUMMER NIGHT WITH AUNT GERT

We are walking from the last trolly stop to Savin Rock, the amusement park two blocks away. I am eight years old and am with my older sister and Aunt Gert. The wind sweeps in odors of the ocean, cotton candy, hot dogs, and fried fish, along with the noise of the crowd.

beyond the park lights–
the growing darkness
of the sea

The fat lady with her maniacal laugh stands at the entrance to the fun house. Too scared to go in; too scared to wait outside alone.

sneaking a peak
in the darkened tunnel–
eyes half shut

Any ride we want, my aunt says. The giant Ferris wheel, caterpillar, bumper cars. Rides my father would not allow.

screams and laughter
on the roller coaster–
which is mine?

I try games of chance and skill. The penny toss, spin the wheel, pop the balloons. Have neither skill nor luck and leave with no prize and a long face. "Cheer up," my aunt says. "Time for one more ride."

The merry-go-round. The best for last. I choose a big black and white horse. An outside horse, one that moves up and down. No stationary animal for me. Gaining speed. The calliope pumping a tune, quick and gay. I reach for the brass ring. Arms way too short. Next year, I think.

head held back
whirling into the wind
a taste of sea salt

SQUABBLES

We have them often, my sister and I. Not surprising. We are children. Aunt Jo and Uncle Zeb have squabbles, too. Brother and older sister. Not long after Jo moves next door to Zeb, a fence goes up, a long fence all the way down to the road. They are not speaking. Sometime later, a gate appears near the houses. All is well between them.

Through the years, that gate is either open or locked. When open, we visit both Jo and Zeb. We can go from one to the other easily to play with our cousins. When locked, and visiting Jo, my sister and I meet Zeb's boys across the street on the beach.

Different personalities and lives. Jo, with only one child late in life, and Zeb, eventually having four children. In Jo's house, there is order and highly polished floors and no shouting. In Zeb's house there is spilled popcorn and sawdust tracked in from where the chickens are kept in the yard and Aunt Agnes playing the piano.

Mom, younger than Jo, older than Zeb, is caught in the middle. She is mediator and peacemaker. Sometimes, weeks pass with us not visiting either of them.

family feud
the white flag goes up, comes down
becomes tattered;
to take sides or be neutral
children watch and question

MUFFINS

A Sunday morning. Mid-winter. It's snowing and frigid cold outside. It's certain we shall be stuck inside. Mom lets us sleep, my sister and me. With our bedroom just off the kitchen the cooking odors slip through the partially open door.

I sniff the air. Muffins. Hot, fresh, home baked muffins. As many as I can eat. Two, three…maybe four.

The kitchen is warm with heat coming from the oven as well as the oil burning stove. On the table are a bowl of muffins, a tub of butter, a jar of grape jam and the Sunday paper. Mom places in front of me a small plate, a knife and a cup of latte café. The rest is up to me.

full stomach
scattered on the comics
buttered crumbs

NIGHT TERRORS

It starts as a low moaning that quickly escalates into a loud scream.

"Daddy's having a bad dream," my sister says.

From the other end of the flat, the sounds continue. It is not unfamiliar, this night terror. It has happened before. Pressures of the job, financial worries, health concerns. At the time, I know none of this. His screams are beyond my understanding.

They stop abruptly. Voices from my parents' bedroom. Footsteps. A light goes on in the kitchen. My father heating up some milk.

"Go back to bed," he tells my sister who stands in the doorway. "It's O.K.."

I don't want to see him, this man who cries out in the darkness. This man who sits me on his lap and gives me piggy-back rides. This man who buys me ice-cream and sweets from the corner shop. This man is a fearful stranger. I huddle under my blankets imagining terrors more horrible than those that caused his nightmare.

darkened house –
fingers of moonlight
across the floor

SPRING CLEANING

Hot water and vinegar sting my nose. She tells me to rub until the window squeaks. We put lemon wax on the mahogany furniture, polishing until it glows. Not because of company coming, but because it's her way. With the sun on her back, she pulls the just washed curtains taut to fit the stretcher, moving from tack to tack.

the pulse of spring
nimble fingers
find a rhythm

MOM'S WAFFLES

Not just for breakfast. On occasion, for supper. A hot summer night clamors for something refreshing, something cool and fun. Waffles with ice cream. Vanilla, chocolate, strawberry or Neapolitan.

old world Italian
but with visions of the New
she found a way
to blend and create for us
a path into the future

PARTNERS IN CRIME

After dinner, our parents and grandparents are cooling off on the porch. Big Sis and I are upstairs in our bedroom playing checkers. The window is open to catch any breeze. For once, we don't squabble over the game. Suddenly, she flaps her hands, jumps up, sending checkers and board flying, and screams. I am only five years old, and I scream even louder, although I don't know why. She runs around in circles, her arms waving back and forth. I do what she is doing.

"Oh, my God!" Mom stands in the doorway. "Are you hurt?"

"A moth," Sis cries. "A moth on my face."

Something heavy thumps on the floor. It's Dad, fallen in a dead faint.

family reunion
the different versions
of stories we tell

SUMMER OF 1944

Daily headlines in the local newspaper: POLIO. INFANTILE PARALYSIS. POLIOMYELITIS. Whatever it is called, it's talked about in whispers. Like a dirty story.

Beaches, parks, movie houses, all remain open, but hardly anyone goes. It's in the air; on the benches, on the toilets. Stay home. Stay inside. And, we do.

On one Sunday afternoon, my father can take only so much of my sister and me squabbling and whining. He reasons that with most of New Haven staying home, it would be safe to venture out. And there we are, tripping off to the beach on the open-air trolley. Anticipation mixed with disappointment. Not many passengers. No one singing or laughing.

The beach at Lighthouse Point is nearly empty. Only four or five families. And a lonely lifeguard in his tower. We spread our blanket, yards away from anyone else.

"Stay away from them," my father warns. "Don't play with those children."

We hadn't played with anyone since Billy O'Hara was rushed to the hospital by ambulance two weeks earlier. How sick was he? Rumors rolled down our street like a loose ball. He's dead already. He's alive. He's paralyzed. He's in an iron lung. He's crippled. He's only 10 years old.

low tide water line–
a little girl races
her shadow

TRAPPED

During WWII, in the winter months, schools are closed on every other Friday to save on fuel. A headache for working parents. A boon for kids. Little do we know, that come spring, those missing days will extend the school year to the end of June.

the longest day
a robin flies through
an open window

WINE HARVEST

ripe concord grapes–
in the backyard, a contest
of spitting skins

It is a hot day in early September. My grandfather picks grapes from the arbor to make wine. My sister and I are told to stay out of his way and out of trouble. Grandpa's paisan arrives with additional grapes to supplement the backyard harvest. They work together. By late afternoon several baskets stand in even rows. My mother takes one basket for jelly. The rest will be pressed into juice, strained, bottled and stored in the cellar.

sweat on his brow–
he brushes cobwebs
from last year's bottle

BLACKIE

One day Grandpa brings home a small black dog. We go for the obvious and name him Blackie. The little dog wanders between my grandparents flat on the first floor, our flat on the second floor and the yard. Sometimes he escapes the yard, but always comes back.

One morning, Grandpa tosses Blackie into the cellar and locks the door. Soon, men arrive wearing heavy clothing and thick gloves. They go down the cellar carrying a metal cage and come up with Blackie in it. He growls, snarls, bares his teeth. He drools, a foamy bubbly drool. Claws at the cage. Barks violently. The cage is put in a van with a double lock. Blackie's barking and snarling continue as the van drives away.

full moon
above my head
grasping shadows

THE FIVE AND DIME

Shopping with Mom at Woolworth's is a treat for me. Christmas season is the best. Tinsel and glitter, pine garlands, carols coming from a record player, counters and shelves full of stuff, especially the toy section. Betsy Wetsy dolls, games, shiny roller skates, doll houses.

I want. I want. I want for Christmas, and I want now. A coloring book. Please. Please. A Golden Book. Please. Please.

Wait. Wait. Put it on your list.

The shopping ends with lunch at the counter. Meat loaf with gravy, mashed potatoes and peas served on sand colored crockery with three separate sections. No comingling food, no flooding gravy, no runaway peas.

With a full stomach I am content to wait for the *I wants.*

Christmas ornaments
bought sixty years earlier
from the five-and-dime
the last two swaddled in wool
cradled in wrinkled hands

FABLES AND OTHER YARNS

It's a snow day, and school is closed. I am six or seven years old. My sister and I and our friend, Lena, shovel a clearing in her yard to build a snow man. Whack! I catch the corner of a shovel on my left temple. Sharp pain and a gushing wetness. Blood is streaming in my eyes, down my face.

"I can see your brains," my sister cries.

I believe her and scream. Within seconds, I'm being led, pushed, dragged by Lena's mother into the kitchen. With deft hands she washes the gash, pours on something stinging, pinches the skin together, slaps on a band aid and sends me and my sister home.

shivering tales
spinning memories
and imagination

TREASURE

In the attic of our old house where former lives are stored my sister and I find a locked leather suitcase. We shake it. It rattles with a chinking sound. Coins perhaps? Antique jewelry? Surely, some sort of treasure.

Too heavy to lug downstairs we call Mom who comes with a hammer and chisel.

"Hurry. Hurry. We found it. So, can we keep it?"

With one final fierce blow the lock snaps, and the lid opens. Mom is thrilled.

all day cooking–
mint new canning jars
with gaping mouths

LUNCH WITH GRANDMA AND GRANDPA

Grandpa waits at the kitchen table, while Grandma and I go out to the backyard. We gather the short pale green leaves of a plant before flower buds form and swell on coarse stems and open into the yellow curse of most gardeners who are unaware of the plant's tasty possibilities.

dandelion fluff
a warehouse of wishes
let loose in the wind

The thin, tubular blades have a slightly sharp fragrance, which becomes stronger as we clip, tug and pull up small white bulbs, leaving fingers dirt smeared and aromatic. Back inside the kitchen, we wash the greens, the muddy sludge swirling down the drain. I shake them, my small hand bobbing vigorously next to Grandma's large, rough one. We pat dry them on a towel from the old country, hand woven from wild hemp with strands of brown coursing thru the pale fabric.

treasured objects—
the next generation
hasn't a clue

Grandma chops the greens and a clove of garlic, places them in a bowl with some lemon juice and olive oil, sprinkles on salt and pepper and gives them a toss with a wooden spoon. She fills three plates with the greens, adds chunks of hard cheese, slices of salami and crusty bread. She puts the plates on the table, along with glasses, a carafe of water and a bottle of Grandpa's home-made wine. He pours water into my glass, adds a little wine, and tells me to "mangia."

warm breezes
lazy memories
slip into dreams

GIVE ME ENTERTAINMENT

We listen to the radio. Go to the movies on Saturday afternoons. Have board games and books. In summer, occasional trips to the beach or the amusement park. And, we have the piano.

It is an upright piano and sits in the parlor in my grandparents' downstairs flat. It is a dark reddish brown with even darker streaks throughout. Shiny. Shimmers in the sunlight. My sister and I are not allowed to touch it. Gert plays this piano. We beg and cajole her to play. Doesn't matter what. It's how she plays. The way her hands fly, faster, slower. The way the keys move without her ever touching them. The way her feet pump the pedals. Slowing down, a march becomes a dirge. Speeding up, a waltz becomes a polka.

Stacked on top are the rolls. Wonderous sheets of paper perforated with holes and wrapped around a spool. We watch as Gert opens the sliding door and inserts a roll. She adjusts her posture, her hands, her feet. What will it be tonight? *April Showers; Singing in the Rain; Toot, Toot, Tootsie; The Blue Danube.*

simpler and better
is a question I don't ask
of then versus now
memories adjust by degrees
on a sliding scale

NINE LIVES

The young girl gives it to her mother on Mother's Day. A stray gray and white kitten. How can a mother refuse such a gift? The kitten is named Flossie.

They say a cat has nine lives, and Flossie soon uses up two of them. The first is when she gets into the open garbage pail and retrieves a chicken bone. Choking and gasping, her breath is fast and weak. With quick fingers, the mother forces open Flossie's jaw, reaches in and retrieves the bone.

Shortly thereafter Flossie wanders out an open second floor window onto the sloping roof of the porch below. The fall leaves her spread out flat on the concrete. The young girl screams, "Take her to the vet! Take her to the vet!" The mother picks up the knocked-out kitten, puts her on a bed of towels, and feeds her a small raw meatball laced with a crushed aspirin. Twenty-four hours later, Flossie is frisky as ever and follows her savior everywhere.

One evening, the mother and father go out for a walk, and the girl is told to keep Flossie at home. But . . . the kitten escapes. The parents return, but Flossie does not.

long days of summer
wishing to be young again
to frolic freely
to cancel out all mistakes
to live more than one life

THAT WONDERFUL TOWN

Trips away from home are rare, and always a two-or-three-day visit to New York and to stay at a cousin's house. in the Bronx. A gathering of the clan for a christening, an engagement, a birthday. Manhattan is only a word.

On one summer weekend, after arriving at Grand Central, we walk the familiar underground walk, though long tunnels, but do not board a subway to the Bronx. We keep on walking, footsteps and voices echoing and suitcases getting heavier, until we reach a large glass door, framed with wood. Like a jack-in-the-box, we have popped out of the darkness into the light, the light being the lobby of the Commodore Hotel, all glitter and glow, the grandest sight my eyes have ever seen. Checking-in first, then a swift elevator ride to our rooms on the tenth floor.

My father is our guide. Fifth Avenue and Rockefeller Center, St. Patrick's Cathedral, lunch at an automat, where I want more food just to insert the coins again and open the door. After lunch, a subway to the Empire State Building and an elevator ride up to the clouds. However impressive the view is in the distance I am only interested in looking down at the ant world at ground level. The elevator down is stomach churning, and I hold onto my mother's hand. Back to the hotel where my sister and I are spruced up.

We are on the street again and are walking, walking, weaving our way through the Saturday evening crush of people. The sign above a restaurant door flashes Vesuvius, along with an erupting volcano. Inside is like a movie set. More glitter and glow. It's nothing like Jimmie's Clam Shack or Mario's Pizzeria at home. My sister and I are given orders. No squirming, no bickering. I'm too awned to do either.

My father hails a taxi for our return to the Commodore and sleep, which is slow to come. Taxi horns and sirens—Manhattan's music and not the nightly music of crickets and trees swishing keeps me awake. Sunday morning and a pancake breakfast at Child's restaurant. A subway ride to Canal Street, where my mother shops the sidewalk vendors. Back to mid-town, the automat again for lunch and one more wonderous treat—a movie and stage show at the Roxy—before taking the train home.

doorways to new worlds
chanced upon or guided
need only a hand
a pull on the handle
to enter and explore

COUSINS

1.Clamming

The clams are about 100 yards away, in the sandbar, burrowed deep. We slosh through low water on an ocean floor covered with small, black snails. Rubber swim shoes on my feet. Still feel the bumpy, round, slippery shells, rolling, sliding. My sister and I complain and go slowly. Bobby and Donny, our older cousins, laugh and splash us. They have bare feet and run across.

At seven years of age, I'm the youngest and the smallest. The stomper on the sand bar. I punch my heels down. Here. **There!** A shot of water. Quahogs. Piss clams we call them. My cousins and sister dig**!** **Dig!** After a while we change positions, but not for long. My hands too small to dig fast. The clams get away. With our eyes always on the sea level, we fill our buckets.

sunburned bodies–
scrambling on rocks
above the tide

2. Lords of The Sea

Older now. The boys are twelve and thirteen. Slim and lithe, sun brown as walnuts and speed swimmers. Living across from the water, they are out every day on this lonely, narrow and empty stretch of sand beyond a crumbling rock wall. I am not a good swimmer. I splash and dog-paddle, sink and rise to sink again.

low tide
testing courage on the backs
of periwinkles

Beyond the sandbar, beyond the slippery mud and snails, the sea bed is smooth with undulating sand, the water, a pale blue-green, free of sea weed, calm as bath water.

splashing waves
gales of laughter
and a screaming voice

The cousins pull me by the ankles, push me down, four arms against two, flapping and useless. Lungs hurt. Bright lights flashing behind closed eyes. Fear.

a bad dream
mama brings sunshine
into the night

The sea in my mouth, the sudden rise to air filling my lungs. As I stand gasping, crying, tears mingling with salt water, the boys move away.

tide coming in
the rush to safe land
and life as normal

CENTER STAGE

I'm shy, a little overweight and wear glasses. I'm smart, but I don't raise my hand in class. I don't volunteer to read aloud. I don't want to be included in a class play, even as the narrator reading from a script. I'm not like my older sister who relishes being center stage. When appointed to be the narrator, I'm too scared to object. I practice reading the lines at home, again and again. My sister is my audience. Rehearsals go smoothly; there's only the teacher and the other kids in the play. On the day of the show, there's lots of encouragement from the teacher and big sis, but now there is an audience.

"You have to do it," my sister says.

"You do it," I say. I give her the script and go sit in the back of the auditorium.

She does it beautifully, not merely reading the narrative, but reciting it from memory.

spring snowfall
daffodil buds delayed
another day

REMNANTS

We call her Crazy Rachel. She may be young, but in our minds, she is old. She wears a red Raggedy Ann wig that fits poorly, exposing lank strands of dull brown hair. Her clothes are loose and baggy, a long skirt and man's jacket, too heavy for the hot summer days when she comes down our street pushing her cart. "Rags, rags. Give me your rags." Our mothers send us outside with bundles collected during the winter months—tattered sheets, paper thin towels, torn clothes, any cloth item that cannot be repaired, reused or recycled.

We toss our bundles into the cart, taking care not to get close to her. "She is a witch," we whisper as we run back to the safety of the sidewalk.

Crazy Rachel doesn't collect many bundles, and, if she does, they are small. It is the war years, and there is little to use and even less to throw away.

Then . . . one summer the war is over. Meat and butter are back on the dinner table. Ration cards become souvenirs. Prosperity is promised for all, and Crazy Rachel no longer comes down our street. Her call of "Rags, rags," becomes just a memory.

hidden lives
huddled in the shadows
beyond our ken
a blink on our horizon
we ignore and soon forget

WHAT I DID LAST SUMMER

It won't cost much, I say. Two weeks at a YWCA summer camp. Just one week? I get the two weeks. I'm twelve years old and this will be the first time away from family. I pack clothing, toiletries and bedding. Uncle Jimmie drives me and my parents to the campground and we are given a tour.

There are six log cabins and a lodge arranged in a circle around a large open space. Eight girls, including a junior counselor, to a cabin. Metal bunk beds with thin mattresses. A covered area with tables and benches and a brick fire pit. A shower building behind the lodge and outhouses in the trees.

We are assigned our cabins and given a schedule with a list of rotating chores: gather firewood, help cook meals, clean up, and a list of activities. I know only a couple of girls from the weekly meetings at the Y, but they are not with me. I begin to have doubts about staying.

the hidden moon—
squeaking hinges
on the outhouse door

cold lake
swimming into
goose bumps

After a few days, I have a friend and the strangeness is not so strange. Half way into the second week we are taken on a hike long after supper, long after the ten p.m. lights out. Told only "Something special" We stop at a clearing, sit on the ground, look up and wait.

a church window
streaks of green, blue, purple
in the night sky

Twenty minutes of awed silence, then a whispering walk back to the cabins. A few days later I’m home.

familiar routine
now and again
a flash of color

AN INTRODUCTION

There are a few Black children in my eighth-grade class. Colored was the word used then. I was sort of friends with Ruth. We hung out at recess and walked part of the way home together. One day Ruth asks me to her home. My grandmother will be annoyed when I come home late, but I say yes, I'll come.

I expect a single-family house or a two family one, like the one I live in. The building, one in a street of such buildings, has four levels. The paint is peeling and the railing is broken.

A few people and kids are in the street, and they are colored. I'm in a colored neighbored, a new experience for me. There is bare dirt in front of the buildings, unlike my grandfather's neat plantings of roses and hydrangeas. I follow Ruth on worn and uneven steps up to the third floor through dun-colored halls, smelling of food and noisy with crying babies and shouting voices. I'm beginning to regret I came.

Upon entering the flat I see an old woman, Ruth's grandmother, scrubbing the raw wood floor on her hands and knees. Unsure of what to do, I look around: a wooden table with a linoleum top, scrubbed wooden counters neatly arranged, white curtains floating on the breeze coming through an open window. There is the fragrance of baking, and I see a plate of buns on the table. Ruth's grandmother stands up, smiles and motions me to sit down.

one cactus blossom
a bee finds the sweet spot
in the center

"Now ain't this nice. Ya brought a playmate home wit ya, Ruth. Sit. Sit and have some biscuits."

This is another new experience. Not the crusty rolls or chunks of Italian bread I know, but something soft, and light.

"Ah'll get some butter and honey and milk. Ah allus have somethin fresh baked fo my little girl afta school. What's ya name, child?"

I tell her and say thank you for the biscuits, eating three, keeping up with Ruth. We don' talk, just eat, quietly sitting in that kitchen smelling of soap and baking. There are more biscuits in the oven which the grandmother watches as we eat. When we finish, not sure if I should stay or go, my timidity gets the better of me. I murmur another thank you and leave.

I do not go there again, or do I invite Ruth to my home, but we still hang out at recess and walk part of the way home together. After graduation that June, we never see each other again.

graduation day
by mid-afternoon
excitement fades

SINGING CHRISTMAS MASS

The first Mass on Christmas at St. Anthony's Church is at 6:00 a.m. I am 13 years old and sing in the choir. It is still dark and my father is already up.

“No breakfast for me," I say. "I'm taking communion."

He has his coffee and a chunk of bread and says he's coming with me.

"Why?" I ask.

"It's dark outside. It's not safe.”

My father never goes to church. Although raised as a Catholic, he often questions the church's authority and the demands placed upon the parishioners. Will he come inside? I try to picture him kneeling, bowing his head, praying, sitting through the sermon.

I'd rather be alone. I'm not a baby. But I say nothing.

first light
his protective hand
when crossing the street

After a twenty-minute walk we reach St. Anthony's. The church, decorated with pines and poinsettias, is not fully lighted, just the vestibule and the choir loft. My father sees me up to the loft and gives me money to buy rolls at the Jewish bakery on the way home.

"You're not staying?" I ask.

"No. It won't be dark after Mass. You'll be O.K. coming home."

Relieved, yet disappointed, I join the other choir members.

believing—
unasked questions floating
with the dust moats

Lights come on in the sanctuary, candles are lighted, the heat is turned on. Mass begins with the church barely half-filled.

voices sing out
through stained glass windows
the rising sun

Beams of color travel over pillars and pews. The organ swells; our voices blend harmoniously; the fragrance of pine boughs, candles and incense float up to the choir loft as our voices soar out over the congregation.

the sun in my eyes
singing "Gloria"
from memory

BEST FRIENDS

Bobbie lives two houses away. She is one year younger, and the only girl on the block closest to my age. We walk to school together, go to Mass together, play together after school and on the weekends. Her family is Polish; mine is Italian Occasionally, I have supper at her house or she at ours. The food is different, and the meal is always awkward. We are polite, both taught to mind our manners and eat whatever is put before us.

It is not the custom to call on the telephone, knock on a door or ring the bell. You stand outside the friend's house and call out the name, a long, drawn-out call.

Ohhhh Bobbbb bieee!"

Ohhhh, Aaaa ddieeee!"!

until someone comes to the window—an adult who sends you away—or the friend comes outside.

We play hopscotch, jacks, trade comic books. We talk about boys, and, in whispers, her aunt's pregnancy.

After I move away, we write regularly for a few years, then just Christmas cards, then nothing. Decades later, I learn that at age twenty-six she passed away from cancer.

black and white photos
our first communion dresses
and smiling faces
time stopped her aging
in exchange for a life

SOCK HOP

Friday night. I'm wearing a circle skirt, puffed out with a crinoline petticoat. I meet a couple of girlfriends outside the high school, and we go in together. There's courage in numbers. At the gym, we remove our shoes. Already, there's a jumble, and I place mine neatly off to one side. We stand around and stand around. Helen is asked to dance. Rita is asked to dance. I move to the other side of the room and stand around and stand around. After an hour, I retrieve my shoes.

scrunching leaves
the rhythm I keep
on the walk home

ARRIVERDERCI

The summer air is charged, filled with tension and static. There are daily discussions. The cold winters, my father's current job situation, concerns about his health. In August, the decision is made. We are moving to Los Angeles, land of sunshine. And Hollywood. And glamour. My galloping imagination held in check with the realities of sorting and packing and leaving behind family and friends.

saying good-bye
the soon forgotten promises
to write often

In October, a month after my sixteenth birthday, we leave Daggett Street. The rooms empty, smaller with the furniture gone. The house in need of paint, the arbor, full of grapes that will not be picked. The taxi honks and we depart.

autumn colors
blurring in a swirl of leaves
all the days to come

ACKNOWLEDGEMENTS:

I wish to thank the editors of the following journals for publishing some of the haibun and tanka prose, either as they appear here or in an earlier version.

A Hundred Gourds: Cry Baby, Cry Baby; Muffins; Center Stage; *Bottle Rockets:* Big Sister; Rascatti's Beach; *Cattails:* Spring Cleaning; *Contemporary Haibun Online:* Mom; Seasons of War; Snow Day; Night Terrors; Wine Harvest; Give Me Entertainment; Cousins; Remnants; *Drifting Sands:* Lunch with Grandma and Grandpa; *Failed Haiku:* Partners in Crime; *Frogpond:* The Long Wait,; A Summer Night with Aunt Gert; *Haibun Today:* Dad; You Go First,; Treasure; An Introduction; *Modern Haiku:* Lights Out, *Moonset:* Cousins: *Presence:* Kindergarten;; Family Trips; Sunday Morning with Dad,; The Palace; Summer of 1944; *Ray's Web Page*: A Winter Afternoon; *Shamrock:* A Childhood Christmas; *Simply Haiku:* Nonni; Singing the Christmas Mass; *Stylus Poetry Journal:* Dad; The Old Neighborhood; *World haiku Review:* Blackie

Front cover: New Haven, CT. 1851, Hartley and Whiteford , creators, with permission from the Connecticut Museum of Culture and History

Dad

Mom

Zeb
Grandpa
Grandma
Jo
Mary Lou
Dad
Jimmie
Mom
Agnes
Addie
cousins

Grandma
Grandpa
Gert

Dad
Addie

Addie
Grandpa
Grandma

Addie Mary Lou

Daggett St. 1950
Addie Mary Lou

Daggett St. 2008

www.ingramcontent.com/pod-product-compliance
Lightning Source LLC
Chambersburg PA
CBHW022201160726
48282CB00024B/278
9788119228461